THE
DRINKER'S
COMPANION

The Drinker's Companion

Nicholas Rootes

LONDON
VICTOR GOLLANCZ LTD
1987

First published in Great Britain 1987
by Victor Gollancz Ltd,
14 Henrietta Street, London WC2E 8QJ

Designed by Jonathan Newdick

British Library Cataloguing in Publication Data
Rootes, Nicholas
    The drinker's companion.
    1. Drinking customs
    I. Title
    394.1′3   GT2885

ISBN 0-575-03866-7

Typeset in Great Britain by Dorchester Typesetting Group Ltd

Printed in Italy by Arnoldo Mondadori Editore

Contents

CHAPTER I

The Bottle

Man's need for stimulating liquid refreshment is as old as civilisation and the means for carrying and storing such precious liquors has tested his ingenuity. There would be little use in fermenting grape or grain unless suitable vessels existed to contain the product of our fruitful labours. So, dear reader, as you sit and sip some benevolent concoction poured from the bottle that you take for granted, spare a thought for our ancestors, who had to drink sour wine and stale ale and for generations were the vanguard in the quest for a perfect bottle.

In the early years of the seventeenth century glass vessels were more expensive than gold or silver. Consequently animal skins, leather bottles and stoneware jugs were in common use. Early glass bottles were prized possessions used time and time again. They were stamped with a seal bearing the owner's name. At the court, the 'Yeoman of the Bottales' was an important royal appointment with a wage to match of £5 a year, a considerable sum at the time.

These vessels were free blown in a variety of shapes. The earliest shape was known as 'shaft and globe', followed by an 'onion' shape. The privileged customer of the vintner sent his bottles to be filled with the contents of a butt. Samuel Pepys' Diaries mention his delight in watching several dozen of his newly made seal bottles being filled. He buried them in the ground during the Great Fire of London and retrieved them once the fire had subsided.

The shape of wine bottles evolved according to necessity from the early spherical shapes towards more cylindrical shapes in response to the need for bottles to be 'binned' horizontally. The binning of wine began with the increasing popularity of Port at the beginning of the eighteenth century. Port matures in the bottle and the only way to keep the air out is to use a cork stopper moistened by the contents. The bottle consequently developed into a shape that could easily be laid down.

Bottles come in all sizes. Attempts were made to regulate the measures of wine sold as early as 1662, but this proved impossible as free blown bottles varied so much in size. It was not until the early nineteenth century that bottle moulds began to be used commercially. Until recently Champagne could be found in sizes ranging from a ¼ bottle to a Nebuchadnezzar containing 20 bottles, but nowadays Nebuchadnezzars are very hard to come by, perhaps because of their occasional propensity to explode. The largest bottle ever made was blown in Stoke-on-Trent in 1958. Christened an 'Adelaide', it was five feet wide and held 20½ gallons of sherry.

Spirits began to be drunk in quantity during the eighteenth century. Square glass 'case' bottles containing Gin or 'Geneva' were shipped from Holland packed in wooden crates, but it was not until the following century that Whisky began to be widely appreciated outside Scotland. During the nineteenth century, spirits for export to the colonies were bottled in earthenware jugs with the name of the manufacturer indelibly printed under the glaze. Paper labels would have soon disintegrated on the arduous journey.

The first bottles used for carbonated drinks were invented by William Hamilton in 1809. These lay on their sides in order to moisten the corks, which were tied in position. The name of Hiram Codd is inseparably linked with the development of carbonated drinks. Hardened drinkers used to refer contemptuously to his globe stoppered bottles as 'Codd's Wallop'. The genius of Codd's invention was in the design of the bottle, which was stoppered from inside by a marble that was forced up the neck to close the mouth by the internal pressure of the gas.

The Codd bottle tended to spray its contents over the unfortunate person opening it. Consequent-ly various methods of opening such bottles were devised. Alternative bottle closures to Codd's made little progress until Codd's original patent ran out in 1888, which coincided with the invention of a bottling machine that could produce bottles cheaply with screw lips. In the quest for perfection, bottles were designed with lips that had external threads, internal threads, stud projections, levers and hinged stoppers.

A Tudor Bellarmine bottle, named after the sadistic Cardinal Bellarmine, who persecuted Protestants.

Such bottles were originally produced to drink to his eternal damnation

A Delft ware Sack bottle dated 1649. Sack was an immensely popular wine in Elizabethan England. It was often served sweetened, or hot with an egg and a piece of toast floating in it

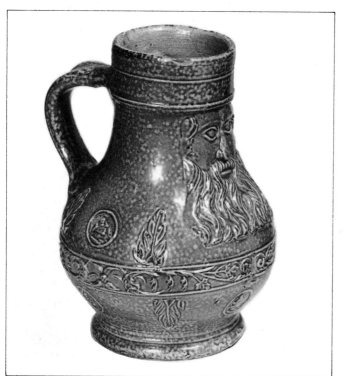

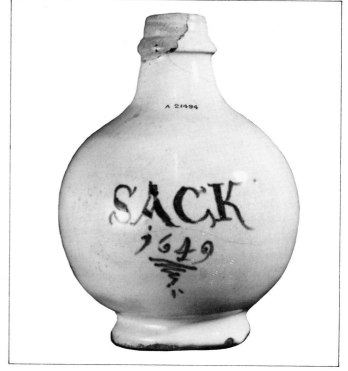

The earliest intact glass wine bottle with a seal and date that has ever been recovered. Dated 1657

A group of antique wine seal bottles. Circa 1680–1700

The development in shape of the cylindrical wine bottle

Bottle sizes – from the right: ¼, ½, single, Magnum (2 bottles), Jeroboam (4 bottles), Methuselah (8 bottles), Salmanezah (12 bottles) and Balthazar (16 bottles)

The 'Butler's Enemy' or
Burns's Patent Bottle Lock
with the original
instructions

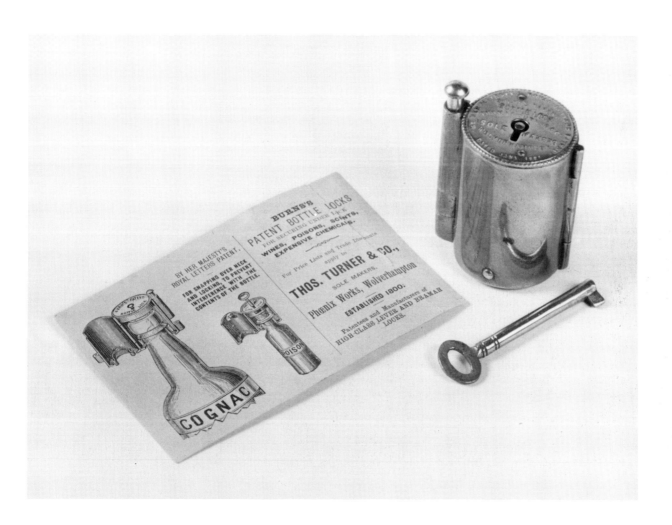

Codd and Rylands valve bottle. Pressure was released through the valve and the stopper then dropped

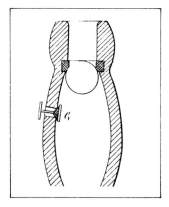

Dan Rylands modified the neck of the Codd bottle so that the marble was held to one side while pouring

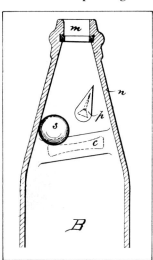

Codd patented this machine for opening his bottles. The lever pushes a flexible rubber ball onto the mouth. This compresses air above the stopper causing it to drop.

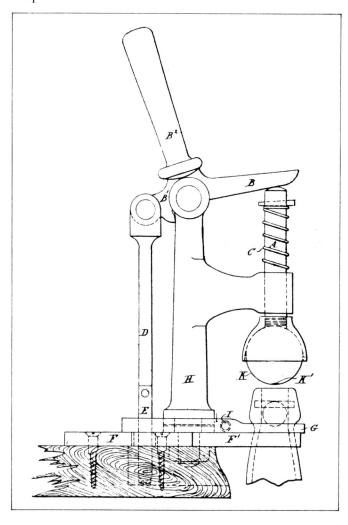

Skerritt's patent screw on bottle stopper with the thread on the outside of the bottle

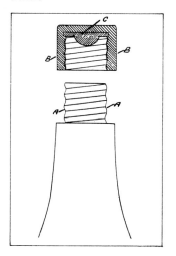

Harrison's patent screw stopper with the thread inside the bottle

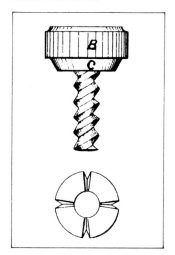

Williams' patent bottle stopper with stud projections that lock into the cap

Marshall's patent bottle stopper with a hinged top lever

Denison's patent hinged stopper

Dan Rylands patent stopper with a notched side lever

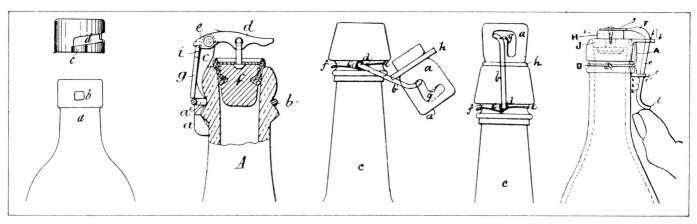

A variety of Codd patent bottles as advertised in L. Lumley's 1897 catalogue of items supplied to the hotel and pub trade

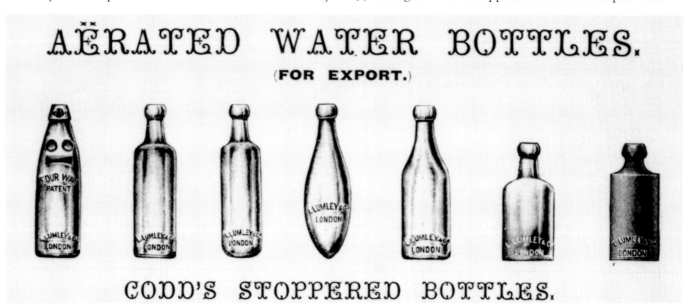

AËRATED WATER BOTTLES.

(FOR EXPORT.)

CODD'S STOPPERED BOTTLES.

A group of silver mounted
bottle corks dating from
1812 to 1905

CHAPTER II

Corks and Corkscrews

A bas–relief of Dom Perignon, his discovery in hand, at the Abbey of Hautvillers

CORKS

Cork is an ideal material for stoppering a bottle as it is impervious to liquid and readily compressible to form an airtight seal. The inner bark of the cork oak *Quercus suber* is used. By reputation, the best cork is produced in Catalonia and Portugal. In Europe, cork replaced oiled hemp during the sixteenth century as a means of sealing bottles. Dom Perignon, a Benedictine monk, was the first to produce a cylindrical cork that formed a truly airtight seal. With the use of stronger bottles, he developed a method of containing the secondary fermentation of wine within the bottle, which is the reason why Champagne has a sparkle.

Another function of the cork is to provide information on the contents of a bottle. It survives long after the decay of a paper label. Vintage Port, which traditionally has no label, is branded on the cork with the name of the shipper and vineyard. Top growth clarets will have all the necessary information including the vintage on the cork.

Corks come in various shapes and sizes. There are long ones for vintage wines and short ones for the everyday variety. Though cylindrical when fitted, Champagne corks splay out under the continuous pressure of six atmospheres contained within the bottle.

CORKSCREWS

'We lost our corkscrew and were compelled to live on food and water for several days!' – W. C. Fields' recollections from a journey to Afghanistan.

We tend to take corkscrews for granted, but it is only after struggling to push in the cork and being squirted in the face by a jet of wine, that the convenience of such an instrument is apparent. Not that every corkscrew offers a foolproof method of extraction. There is the corkscrew that insists on entering the cork off centre, splitting it and crumbling pieces into the bottle. Yet another drills boldly in and pulls straight out through the same hole leaving the cork unmoved. A case of premature withdrawal if ever there was one.

The Reverend Samuel Henshall is famed for being granted the first patent for a corkscrew in 1795. His drawings illustrated two possibilities. First, an apparently simple but ingenious corkscrew, featuring a button on the shank, which turned the cork once the worm was fully inserted, breaking any adhesion to the bottle and compressing the cork. Secondly, he used the same principle within a frame containing a female thread, that made it possible to withdraw the cork by a continued turning of the handle.

With prolific inventiveness Europeans and

A machine for inserting
corks, illustrated in Rees
Cyclopedia of 1820

Attempting to extract a
cork two hundred years ago

Americans became obsessed with devising bizarre
instruments to extract corks. To aid those with the
feeblest of grips, inventors designed corkscrews with
interlocking screws and rack and pinion actions that
removed the need to exert any physical effort.

Corkscrews come in all shapes and sizes to
satisfy all tastes. There are examples of decorative,
concealed, disguised, multi-purpose and plain odd
corkscrews to be found. The humble function of
pulling a cork from a bottle has been elevated by the
art vested in the instruments of extraction, to such an
extent, that some corkscrews command a remarkable
price in the sale room.

Drawings from Henshall's
Patent specification of 1795

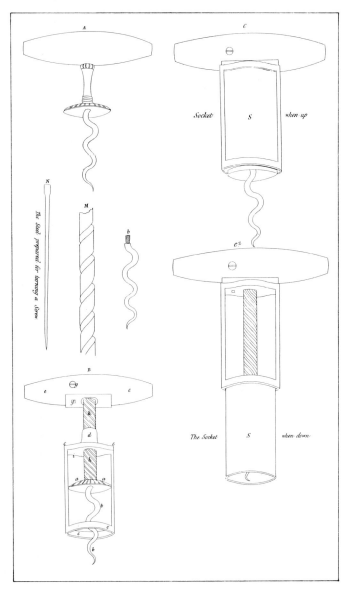

Georgian corkscrews with
similar buttons, one of
which is serrated for a
better grip. Brush handles

first appeared in the late
eighteenth century to dust
off the top of the bottle

A rare German corkscrew
with a spring bell to aid
withdrawal

A cork extractor for
removing pushed-in corks

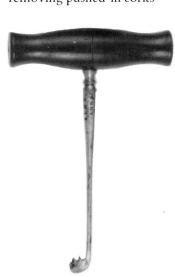

The 'Butler's Friend'; so called because the cork is removed without damage. Hence, The Butler could slake his thirst and top up the bottle with whatever he liked, before reinserting the cork

A concertina action Zig Zag corkscrew

Tongs combining a corkscrew and foil cutter

A double lever corkscrew

A compound Irish harp, containing several different worms and a multitude of tools

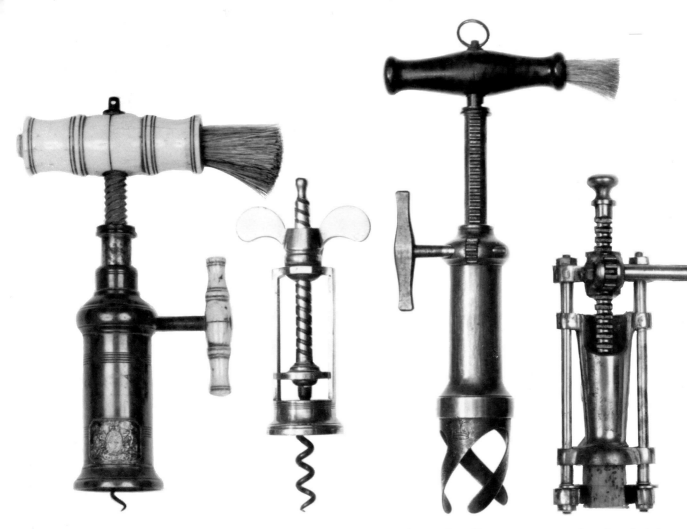

Thomasons 1802 Patent 'Ne-plus-ultra' corkscrew has three screws, the threads of which interact to withdraw the cork by a continued turning of the handle. A reverse turn removes the cork from the worm

A Farrow and Jackson corkscrew of around 1799

Thomas Lund's patent bottle grip of 1838 firmly embraces the neck of the bottle

A rack and pinion corkscrew operated by a side handle

A mid-eighteenth-century combination nutmeg grater, corkscrew in silver

A silver mounted horn-handled bottle opener, corkscrew

A Jensen silver corkscrew

A French ivory corkscrew piqué in brass

A corkscrew disguised as a pig

A corkscrew concealed in the handle of a walking stick

A naughty corkscrew

A piscatorial corkscrew

A very early sheathed silver
corkscrew of around 1680,
decorated with a pair of
fighting cocks. Sold at
Christies for £2,700 in July
1982

A bronze nineteenth-
century English style
corkscrew. Sold at
Sothebys for £4,620 in May
1985

A rare Shrapnel corkscrew invented in 1839 by Henry Needham Scrope Shrapnel, whose father invented the shrapnel shell. Only five known examples exist, one of which was presented to Prince Albert in 1840. Sold at Sothebys for £1,650 in December 1985

Bar corkscrews first appeared in the mid-nineteenth century and were attached to the bar counter to help hard-pressed barmen speed up the process of opening bottles

The Rotary Eclipse. A magnificent brass bar corkscrew made in the late nineteenth century

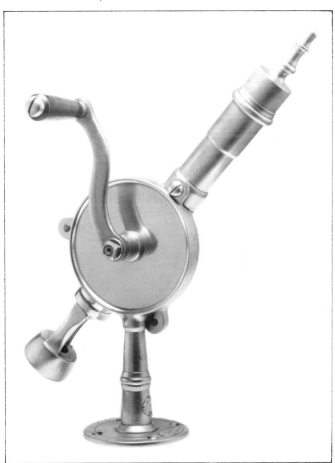

Labels designed for
Château Mouton Rothschild

By Georges Braque

By Joan Miró

By Pablo Picasso

By Marc Chagall

By Henry Moore

CHAPTER III
Labels

'Upon several shelves there stood bottles of all sorts of wine, new and old, with labells pasted upon each bottle, and in order a plenty as I never saw books in a bookseller's shop' – Samuel Pepys, January 19, 1663.

Inundated as we are today with branded products boldly announcing their identity, it is hard to imagine a time when labels were not used. But bottles were not commonly labelled until the binning of wine made it necessary to identify the contents of sleeping bottles. The reference in Pepys' diaries is unusually early as bottled vintage wines were scarce in England before 1730, due to their inability to mature without the use of close fitting corks. Before then bottles carried glass seals, but these identified the owners of such precious vessels, rather than the contents. Initially parchment labels were gummed to the sides of bottles or slipped over their necks, while other bottles were sometimes identified with the use of painted lettering. Enamel and silver wine labels, or bottle tickets as they were then known, emerged when decanters began to be used for serving wine. These labels were hung on chains around the necks of decanters.

Today, a mass of information is revealed on wine labels. A label on a good French wine, for instance, will include details of the Château, the owner, the producer and bottler, the vintage, A.C. region and the contents by volume. In the case of Château Mouton Rothschild, each label is also a work of art. Since 1924, Baron Philippe de Rothschild has commissioned contemporary artists to design the labels and has paid each artist with a case of the vintage for which their label was used and another case from the year of their choice.

Bottled beer began to be produced in quantity to quench the thirst of colonials in the far flung outposts of the British Empire. Paper labels emerged as an efficient and durable method of exhibiting the name of the brewer and the nature of the contents of exported beer. Bass and Co. were the first to produce a mass marketed bottled beer complete with label in 1843, with the launch of their East Indian Pale Ale, an ale specially brewed for the British sweltering in the hot climate of the Indian Continent.

A detail from Hogarth's
'An Election Entertainment'
showing the use of
parchment labels

Rare Battersea enamel wine labels

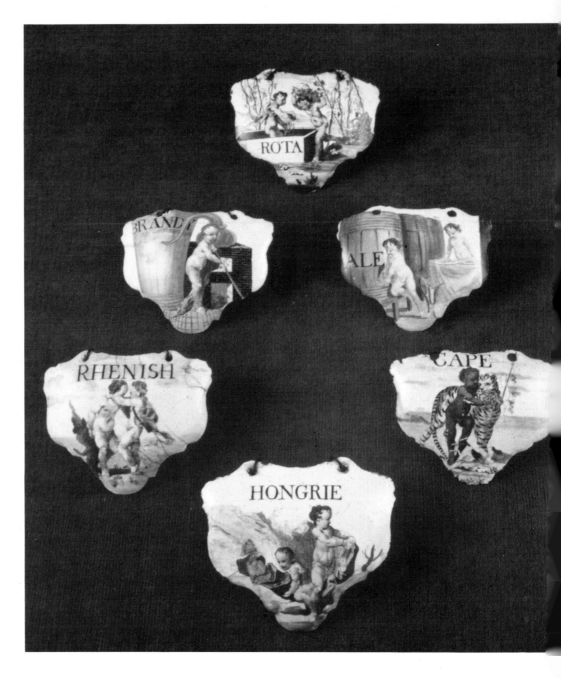

A group of silver wine labels. They are avidly collected and can sell for over £1,000 each if designed by a famous silversmith.

Top row from left to right: Madeira – Charles Rawlings, 1823; Sherry – Paul Storr, 1812; Sherry – Edward Farrell, 1818;

bottom row from left to right: Madeira – Edward Farrell, 1843; Claret – Charles Rawlings, 1831; Claret – Paul Storr, 1816; Sercial – John Reily, 1825

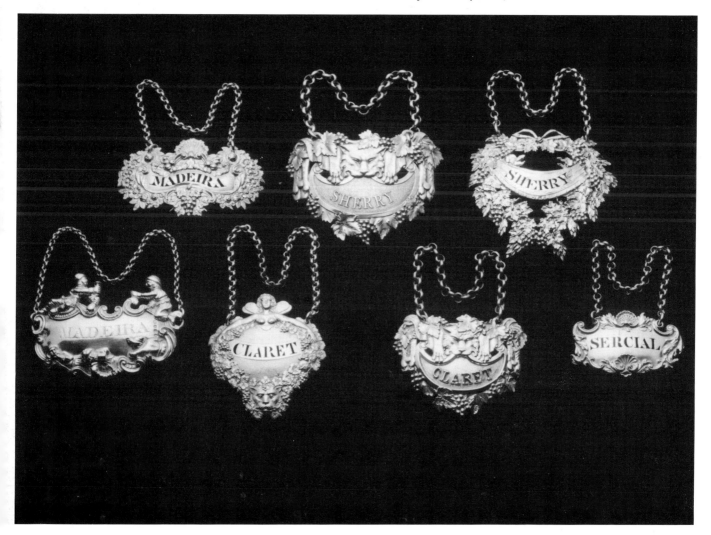

A selection of classic British beer labels

A pre-1900 Tennents Porter label

A Charrington's 'Brown Ale' label of around 1925

The first trade mark ever to be registered, Bass & Co's famous triangle, which was in use before 1875

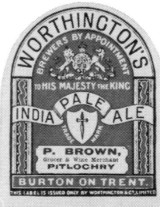

A Guinness Foreign Extra Stout label. Breweries used to leave the task of bottling to each local wholesaler, who then printed his name on the label

A pre-1940 label for Mitchells & Butlers 'Family Ale' showing the charming 'deer's leap' logo, which was used for many years

Worthington's India Pale Ale, brewed by appointment to King Edward. A Royal Warrant was displayed on Worthington labels until 1935

Items illustrated in L. Lumley's trade catalogue of 1897
Right: The bottle cap also provided the opportunity to identify the contents and advertise the name of the supplier
Below: A hand capsuling device

These caves, carved out of chalk by the Romans, run 5 miles underground and are used by Ruinart Père et Fils, the oldest existing Champagne House. The bottles are shown 'en pupîtres'. In this position, they undergo 'remuage', a process whereby the sediment settles in the neck, before being removed during the 'dégorgement', when the bottles are recorked

CHAPTER IV
Notable Bottles

Wine is a living thing. It develops from adolescence to maturity and if not drunk, to weak old age. Before the development of tight fitting corks, its life was short-lived. Vintage years were unknown, as wine kept in casks soon soured through contact with the air.

We must be grateful, therefore, that vintage wine can now be enjoyed. Not only can the taste and bouquet develop in the bottle, but there is less danger of wine being spoiled by the untimely demise of noblemen, who have fallen or been pushed into the cask. The Duke of Clarence, who drowned in a butt of Malmsey, springs to mind, but he was not the first. History relates that Fliolmus, King of the Goths, and a sixth-century Irish monarch met similar fates.

It is surprising how long wine may keep in the bottle. Recently a 1784 bottle of Château Yquem was pronounced sound by some of the world's greatest wine connoisseurs. Much depends on the condition of the cork. The Crus Classés of Bordeaux are re-corked every 25 years, whilst ageing at the Châteaux and, on occasion, a cellarmaster may even travel abroad to re-cork the vintage wine from his Château.

Many old wines have survived due to the foresight of the owners of private cellars. A magnificent cellar recently came to light below a Château in Southern Belgium, which had been occupied by the German High Command during the Second World War. The cellar remained intact, because it had been walled up and concealed by the addition of false wine bins.

What makes a bottle noteworthy? The taste, of course, is imperative, if it is to be savoured, though the most expensive bottles may never be drunk owing to their intrinsic historic value. All the world record prices for single bottles of wine are held by Château Lafite. The rarity of some of their most famous vintages, the longevity of production and of the wine itself accounts for this.

Five of the earliest bottles produced by Moët and Chandon, including the earliest extant bottle of champagne, dated 1741

The world record price for a single bottle is held by this bottle of Château 'Lafitte' dated 1787. The bottle bears the initials of Thomas Jefferson, the third President of the USA and a notable connoisseur of wine. Sold by Christie's in London for £105,000 on 5th December 1985

A bottle of 1806 Château Lafite Rothschild sold by Sothebys in London for £10,780 (including buyer's premium) on 11th December 1985

The former world record holder. $31,000 was paid in the USA for this bottle of 1822 Château Lafite Rothschild, sold by Heublein in 1980

The Macallan, a very fine single malt. Only 350 bottles were filled from three casks after the evaporation of 50 years had taken its toll. The rarity value of these bottles has led to them changing hands for over £500 a bottle

An 1880s bottle of Pimms from the Officers' Mess in Cairo that was reported as being preserved 'to drink to the Memory of Gordon when Khartoum was captured' (*The London Morning Paper*, 23 August 1898)

James Pimms invented the world's first gin sling in the 1840s. His successors

bottled it and supplied it around the world. Only six people within the firm know the complete recipe and they are sworn to secrecy

A bottle of Rémy Martin Très Vieille Grande Champagne in a Baccarat decanter, served at a royal banquet for King George VI and Queen Elizabeth, held at the Château de Versailles in 1938

Useful decanting equipment: Cradle, funnel and decanter. 'The Ultimate' decanting cradle is a modern cradle based on a nineteenth-century design

CHAPTER V

Decanting and Decanters

Coaxing that little genie, the bouquet, from wine has long been one of man's finer aspirations. This fragrance is a timid creature that will shrivel up and hide given half a chance. The object of decanting is not only to leave the sediment at the bottom of the bottle, but also to allow the wine to become sufficiently aerated to release the bouquet.

The first probable printed reference to a decanter was made in an advertisement of 1690 for an earthenware jug with a lip and a handle. Liquid was 'canted' from the original container into a decanter. During the eighteenth century, the growing popularity of port necessitated the use of decanters for separating the wine from the sediment. Early decanters mimicked the shape of bottles and had no stoppers. Wine bottles were often adapted into decanters by the addition of handles and silver or pewter mounts. In time an increasing variety of shapes and sizes of decanters developed. Some, like Ship's decanters, were designed specifically for the exigency of the environment in which they were used, while others showed off the skills of the glass cutter.

Even spirits were frequently decanted, not to improve the liquor but for the sake of appearance and on occasion to provide anonymity for the liquor within. When gin drinking was a national vice in England, genteel Victorians, with a touch of hypocrisy, decanted their gin and labelled it in reverse, 'Nig', so as not to put temptation in the way of their servants.

A wine bottle of around 1680, bearing the glass seal of its owner, converted into a silver mounted decanter

35

An onion-shaped wine
bottle converted into a
decanter by the addition of
a glass handle

An eighteenth-century
'Lynn' decanter. The
horizontal ribbing is a
characteristic of glasshouses
that operated near King's
Lynn in Norfolk

An early eighteenth-
century cruciform decanter,
so called because the
projecting sides are
reminiscent of a cross

A pair of elegant decanters
of around 1790. The ring
necks provide a better grip.
Also, a ship's decanter for
providing solace during a
long voyage. It has a low
centre of gravity for the
additional stability needed
on board ship

A pair of cut glass Regency
decanters with mushroom
stoppers and a 'step and
slice' cut claret jug. The
English have had a long
love affair with claret, ever
since Henry II married
Eleanor of Aquitaine. A
good move, since the
region of Bordeaux was
part of her dowry

A set of spirit decanters,
with engraved labels, in a
silver stand

The Port decanter traditionally travels clockwise around the table. Should a guest fail to pass it on, he should be admonished with the cry 'Bishop of Norwich', a member of the clergy who achieved notoriety for failing to pass the port

A set of 6 toasting glasses and a port decanter dating from the middle of the eighteenth century

Claret jugs with sporting themes

Engraved with a hunting
scene and embellished with
an enamel cap for a lid

Engraved with runners in
an eternal race around the
circumference of the jug

A transport of delight

A pair of Georgian
decanters on a mid-
nineteenth century Sheffield
plate decanter trolley

On occasion, the need has arisen to lock up or even conceal the decanter, perhaps to keep the butler at bay, or to conceal the best brandy from a bibulous house guest.

A selection of locking and concealed decanters from a 1930s Asprey catalogue

Cut glass decanters with spring locks

A silver plated spring lock Tantalus with two cut glass decanters. The Tantalus, which firmly secures the decanters, is named in memory of King Tantalus. As a punishment for revealing the secrets of Zeus, he was immersed up to his chin in water and 'tantalised' with the sight of fine fruits, that always remained out of reach.

CUT GLASS DECANTERS

FINE BOLD HEAVY PLAIN
GLASS DECANTERS

Capacity
¾ pint
1 pint
2 pints

SILVER PLATED SPRING LOCK
TANTALUS

Fitted with 2 English Cut Glass
Decanters

£9 10 0

A silver gilt mounted decanter with a lockable stopper, made in the form of a Champagne bottle around 1820, standing in a silver plate wine cooler

Many a lengthy dissertation has been composed on the subject of decanting and the tools needed to perfect the art. Since the slightest slip might allow the sediment to escape the bottle, decanting cradles that tilt mechanically, were devised to aid the shaking hand

Three styles of decanting cradle

The functional

The naturalistic

The expedient, having a compartment for useful implements set in the case

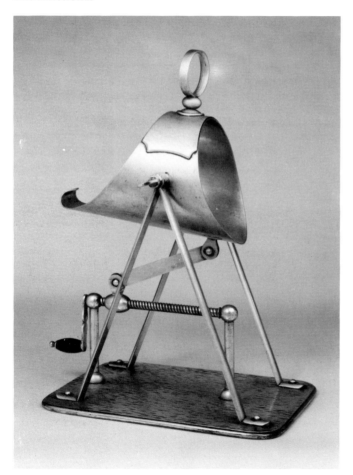

Further devices to assist in the art of decanting

A bottle holder, for steady pouring

A decanting syphon that belonged to the Prince Regent, dated 1805

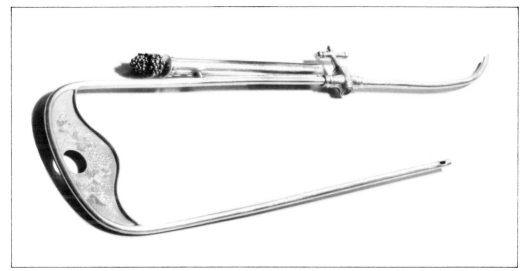

Five silver wine funnels. The cranked spout of a funnel assists the flow of wine against the side of a decanter. The rim is often detachable so that a muslin straining cloth can be fitted

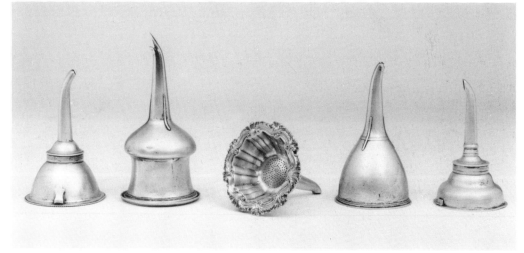

This tantalus, presented to Dr A. J. E. Parker in 1899 by the grateful patients of Easington Lane, Hetton-le-Hole, contains spirit decanters, glasses, ashtrays, a humidor for cigars and a mirror in the lid

After the hunt, the exhausted protagonists would slouch in front of a blazing fire, glasses in hand, facing the dilemma of who should stir to pass the decanter.

Necessity is of course the mother of invention, and so the semi-circular hunt table was born. Situated in front of the fireplace, and with a fire shield to protect the decanters, the table is fitted with a decanter carriage, which pivots on rollers around the circumference of the table.

A William IV mahogany
hunt table

One of the earliest drinking glasses made by a Venetian in England. A glass goblet made in London by Jacopo Verzelini in 1586

CHAPTER VI

Drinking Vessels

Four hundred years ago, it would have been necessary to travel to Venice to find a decent drinking glass. Instead, man quenched his thirst with the help of tankards and other vessels made in a great variety of materials.

The Venetians pioneered the production of cristallo drinking glasses from the middle of the fifteenth century. The secrets of glassmaking were so closely guarded that glassmakers were forbidden to travel abroad. However, in a spirit of free enterprise, Venetian glassmakers defected to the North, seeking fame and fortune. The first to arrive in England was Jacopo Verzelini, who was granted a patent by Queen Elizabeth I to produce cristallo drinking glasses 'à la façon de Venise'.

By the beginning of the seventeenth century, English glasshouses were burning so much wood that a contemporary source claimed that it was ' . . . A lesse evill to reduce the times unto the ancient manner of drinking in stone, than to waste the country's forests'. But despite the establishment of an English glassmaking industry, drinking glasses from Venice remained the most sought after. The surviving letters of a glass seller, John Greene, show that he ordered 24,000 drinking glasses from Venice in five years between 1667 and 1672, to at least 173 specified patterns.

An Englishman, George Ravenscroft, experimented with the constituents of glass and developed lead glass, which was stronger than Venetian cristallo. In 1676, the glass sellers' Company allowed him to use the 'Raven's head' seal. The characteristics of lead glass were shown to best effect in plain drinking glasses with baluster stems.

Since glass was extremely expensive, many drinking glasses were used indiscriminately for whatever drink was to hand. However, with the increasing sophistication of society, glasses for specific purposes were developed.

A sixteenth-century goblet
decorated with gold leaf
and made either in Venice,
or in the Southern
Netherlands à la façon de
Venise

Tankards made in a variety of materials

A sixteenth-century
stoneware jug

An early seventeenth-
century birchwood mazer
from Norway

A silver tankard of 1645

An English glass tankard of
the late seventeenth century

A seventeenth-century
Norwegian silver tankard
standing on ball and claw
feet

Two pages from John Greene's specifications for drinking glasses from Venice

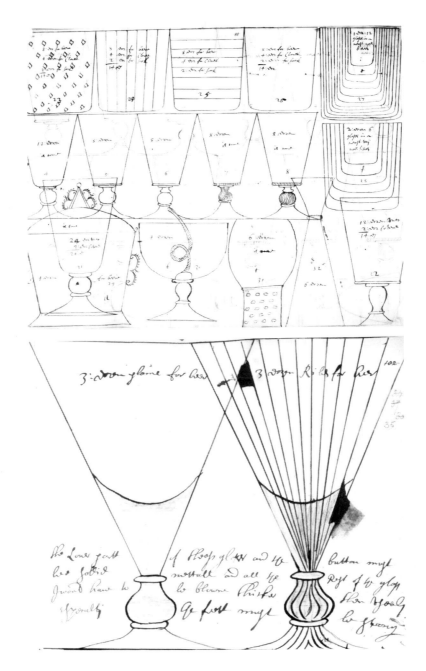

Left: A tankard made of Venetian glass mounted in silver gilt and hallmarked 1546/7. This would have been a highly prized possession at a time when glass drinking vessels were rare in England

Cristallo Venetian drinking
glasses of the sixteenth and
seventeenth centuries.
Drinking glasses with
elaborately constructed
stems cost five times more
to produce than plain
stemmed ones

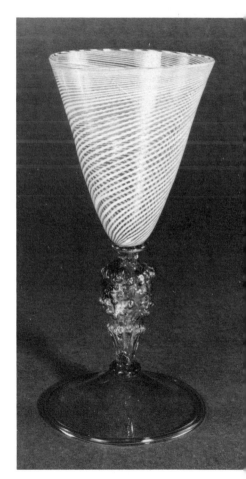

Almost unique to survive as
a set are these 6 English
baluster wine glasses of
around 1710

In England as early as 1531, legislation was passed to standardise the capacities of ale vessels and many a prosecution followed for the sale of short measures. A regular supply of inexpensive ale was of such importance to the political stability of the country that brewers were ordered to produce an adequate supply for the populace. Their breweries were confiscated if 'The King's subjects should bee destitute or unprovided of drynke'.

In the eighteenth century, ale, frequently heavily spiced, was far stronger than the equivalent today. Consequently, it was drunk from comparatively small glasses. 'Small' beer was the after brew of the malt and was weak enough to be drunk throughout the day. The average working man drank three or four quarts a day, starting in the early morning. Water was not safe to drink.

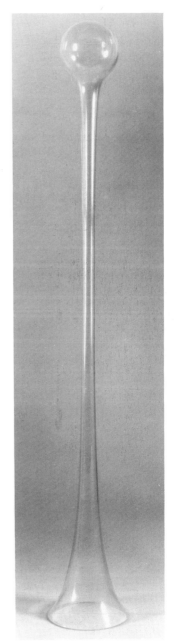

Above: A ½ yard of ale glass

Right: A yard of ale glass

Left: Glasses for strong ale. Far left: A short ale glass of around 1720. Middle and right: Two eighteenth-century ale glasses appropriately engraved with hops

55

Two types of Champagne glass. On the left, with a coupe bowl, circa 1750, and on the right, a Champagne flute of around 1780. Described as the 'witty liquor', on account of its tendency for loosening the tongue, Champagne was first introduced to London society by an urbane Frenchman, Le Chevalier de St Evremond, who was exiled from France by Louis XIV

A Ratafia flute (left) and a Cordial glass, both made around 1750. Cordials were precursors of the modern cocktail and consisted of fruits, herbs and spices infused with alcohol. Ratafia was a brandy-based cordial, flavoured with sugar, spices and either apricots or cherries

A large Georgian beaker of around 1750. Admiral Vernon, nicknamed 'Old Grog', in reference to his grogram coat, incensed British sailors by ordering the dilution of their rum rations with water. Henceforth, the watered-down liquor became known as 'Grog'

A Georgian toddy lifter and a barrel-shaped goblet. In 1694, Admiral Edward Russell threw a party of such scale, that punch was served from a fountain by a boy in a boat floating on the concoction. It provided liquid sustenance for 6,000 guests

Some glasses were made for the requirements of a particular occasion

A firing glass of around 1775, so called because the sound of numerous glasses being hammered on the table in approval of a toast resembled musket fire. Consequently such a glass was constructed with a solid foot and a strong stem

A deceptive toastmaster's glass. The bowl is almost solid, but gives the impression that the toastmaster is drinking as copiously as his guests

Glasses with opposing political messages

A glass engraved with the Horse of Hanover and inscribed 'Liberty' (from the Stuarts)

A Jacobite 'Amen' glass that sold for £8,000 at Christie's, London, in 1980. Such a glass is inscribed with a Jacobite hymn and refers to James Edward Stuart as James VIII of Scotland

A toasting glass. The stem was made very thin so that the glass could be snapped after a single toast, to prevent it being used for a baser purpose

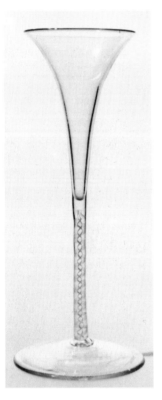

The style of drinking glasses reflects the tastes of each period

A naturalistically styled Victorian Liqueur set. The decanter masquerades as a bird and the glasses as acorns

Part of a set of Lalique glasses and a decanter of Art Deco design

The Cocktail bar at the
Trocadero, London,
around 1930

CHAPTER VII

The Bar

The development of the bar, as we think of it today, began with the gradual introduction of the bar counter. During the nineteenth century, drink was generally served through a hatch from the 'Tap room', where the casks were kept. Bar counters first appeared in urban premises where customers drank standing up. In big cities such as London and Birmingham, bars began to be fitted with machines for the speedier dispensation of liquor. The introduction of beer pumps allowed casks to be conveniently stored in the cellar. Less room was needed behind the counter, allowing more space for customers on the other side.

In England, competition between gin shops and beer houses improved the image of both. The Gin Palace was born, embellished with plate glass windows and a profusion of gas lights, in an attempt to attract a growing middle class. The increasing preoccupation with social status influenced the interior design of public houses. Different classes segregated themselves into different bars. Fittings were developed to make each bar more private, concealing the drinker to an extent, both from the staff and also from the patrons of another bar.

By the end of the nineteenth century, the British were beginning to adapt to the concept of the American or Cocktail bar that served every conceivable mixture of drink. But bars remained the domain of males right up to the First World War. By the end of the War, the outlook was more emancipated. Cocktails like Ragtime were a transatlantic novelty and cocktail bars succumbed to a new generation of 'bright young things'.

A turn-of-the-century design for a bar counter

A sectional view of a beer engine with the casks stored conveniently in the cellar, designed around 1875

Design of an early beer engine illustrated in *Machinery Magazine*

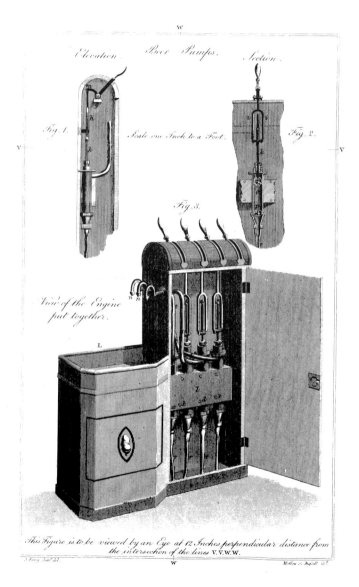

Wine dispensers of the late nineteenth century

A coin operated automatic
Malaga wine dispenser of
around 1890

A Farrow & Jackson
reversible bottle stand

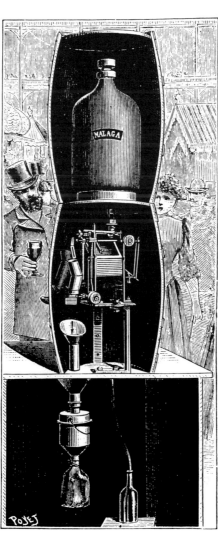

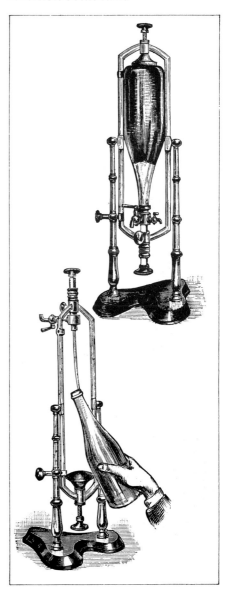

Items for behind the bar
advertised in L. Lumley and
Co's trade catalogue of 1897

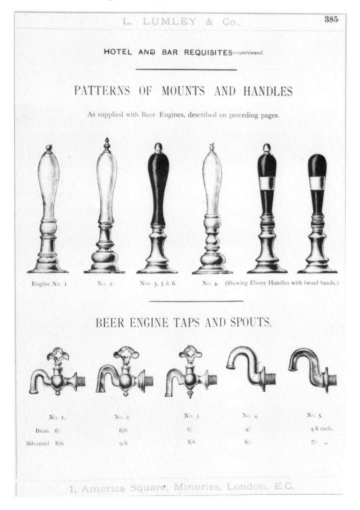

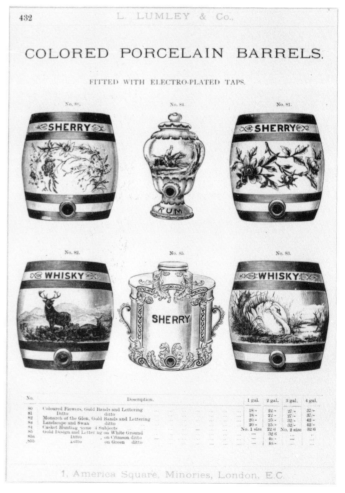

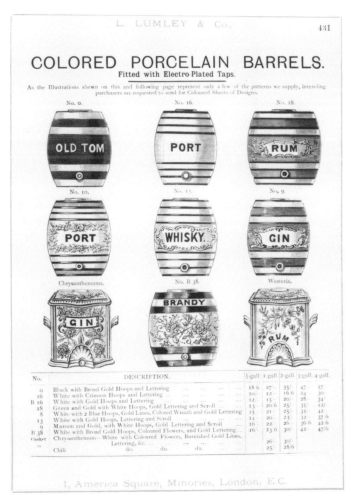

COLORED PORCELAIN BARRELS.
Fitted with Electro-Plated Taps.

As the Illustrations shewn on this and following page represent only a few of the patterns we supply, intending purchasers are requested to send for Coloured Sheets of Designs.

No. 0.   No. 16.   No. 18.

OLD TOM   PORT   RUM

No. 10.   No. 13.   No. 9.

PORT   WHISKY.   GIN

Chrysanthemums.   No. B 38.   Westeria.

GIN   BRANDY   RUM

No.	DESCRIPTION.	½-gall	1 gall.	2-gall.	3-gall.	4-gall.
0	Black with Broad Gold Hoops and Lettering	18 6	27 -	35/-	47 -	57 -
16	White with Crimson Hoops and Lettering	10/-	12 -	16 6	24 -	30/-
B 16	White with Gold Hoops and Lettering	12/-	15 -	20/-	28 -	34/-
18	Green and Gold with White Hoops, Gold Lettering and Scroll ...	13 -	20 6	25/-	35/-	42/-
8	White with 2 Blue Hoops, Gold Lines, Colored Wreath and Gold Lettering	15 -	21 -	25/-	35/-	42 -
13	White with Gold Hoops, Lettering and Scroll	14 -	20 -	24 -	32 -	37 6
9	Maroon and Gold, with White Hoops, Gold Lettering and Scroll ...	16 -	22 -	26 -	36 6	42 6
B 38	White with Broad Gold Hoops, Coloured Flowers, and Gold Lettering...	16 -	23 6	30/-	42 -	47/6
Casket	Chrysanthemum— White with Coloured Flowers, Burnished Gold Lines, Lettering, &c.			26/-	30/-	
"	Chili do. do. do.			25/-	28/6	

IMPROVED TILTING MEASURE.
Can be fixed to any Taps.

EMPTYING MEASURE

Price,
3, 4, 4½, and 5 out,
Nickel Plated, 10/6 each.

SET SCREW

SANDWICH STANDS & COVERS.

GREEN GLASS BOTTLES.

LONG ARM TAP.

9in., 7/6; 10½in., 9/-; 12in., 12/6.

ELECTRO-PLATED SANDWICH TONGS.

For use with Urns or Barrels, when placed on a shelf.
Plated, 9/6.

5/-, 7/6, and 10/-

Fitted with Brass Tap.

½-Gall.		5/-	3-Gall.		10/-
1	,,	6/	4 ,,		12/-
2	,,	9/	5 ,,		15/-

THE BARMAN

That long suffering and often much maligned breed, the barman, is a species that confirms Darwin's 'Theory of Evolution'. Uniquely adapted to his environment, he can perform the most amazing feats of physical agility, while acting a hundred other roles. Showing the patience of Job, he must be prepared to play the part of father confessor and confidant for the midnight ramblings of revellers, whose tongues are loosened by his comforting concoctions.

Mr Robert Burton, head bartender at the Ritz Hotel, London

An American barmaid circa 1894. Her required role was to display her plumage but remain unruffled

An advertisement for Mr T. B. Simpson's American bar in London, dropped from a hot air balloon on 26th July 1859 to publicise its opening

CHAPTER VIII

Mixing It

It would be dogmatic to pinpoint a time when drinks first began to be mixed. They have always been mixed. The Anglo-Saxons mixed liquor in church bells to dispel fiends. The Elizabethans mixed wine with sugar and spice and floated eggs and toast in it. The Georgians made cordials by macerating fruit in brandy and bottling it. But to equivocate, the beginning of mixed drinks in the modern sense started in America, where during the nineteenth century, bars began to serve a plethora of mixed drinks. Cobblers, Juleps, punches, flips, slings and nogs, all passed across the bar counter. Then, of course, there emerged the cocktail, that darling of the Jazz age. Reference can be found to the cocktail as early as 1806 in America, where it was described as a 'stimulating liquor, composed of spirits of any kind, sugar, water and bitters' and 'an excellent electioneering potion'. More specifically, a cocktail is a short drink based on a predominant spirit.

Shaken or stirred? No doubt many a spirited discussion has taken place over this issue. In principle, drinks that must remain undiluted and unclouded by melting ice should be stirred, while a shaker is imperative for drinks that contain ingredients that do not mix easily. Shaking, of course, is more fun. Cocktails are usually mixed as required, though the idea of purchasing a ready-mixed cocktail in a bottle is not new. Such 'branded' products were being sold around the turn of the century.

Bitters, made from herbal and other essences, became popular additions to mixed drinks, particularly as they were purported to have medicinal properties. The Chinese have recently developed a new mixer according to the official newspaper *China Daily*. It is 'essence of earthworm', brewed from earthworms pickled in alcohol. The liquid is claimed to taste good and improves the health.

Soda water was originally developed to mimic spa waters. Sailors were among the first regular drinkers. In 1767, Henry Cavendish devised a means of impregnating water with gas, in order to mimic naturally sparkling mineral water. Five years later, the Admiralty began installing machines that aerated water on board ships, to make distilled water more palatable to ship's crews. Now, soda water is of course a frequent addition to mixed drinks. Fortunes have been made from putting bubbles into water. Jean Jacob Schweppe arrived in London in 1792 and opened a factory producing soda water in Drury Lane. His company went from strength to strength.

Professor Jerry Thomas
mixing his famous 'Blue
Blazer', a combustible
potion, based on whisky,
that is tossed from one
tumbler to another

The father of the cocktail, Jerry Thomas's name is
described in the 1862 edition of his book *The Bonvivant's
Companion*, as being 'synonymous in the lexicon of mixed
drinks with all that is rare and original'

In England, after the First
World War, dinner guests
began to arrive half an hour
early so that the butler
could serve cocktails

Old branded cocktail labels

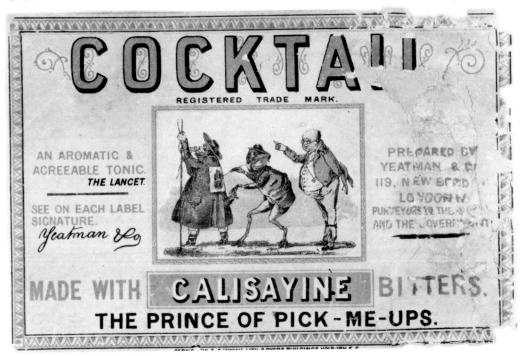

Early Schweppes soda syphons. A nineteenth-century Gazogene syphon and coloured ginger and lemonade syphons used between the two World Wars

Schweppes cordials: 'OT', advertised as 'The Sauce of Drinks', used as a mixer for beer and spirits and launched in 1909. Also grape and ginger brandy cordials

An early American soda fountain counter. The cistern on the top left contains soda water and is packed around with ice. The fountain in the middle dispenses soda, which is flavoured with a choice of syrup

REQUISITES FOR AMERICAN AND ICED DRINKS.

BEVERAGE MIXERS.

For Making Sherry-Cobblers, Mint-Juleps, Brandy-Smashes, Milk-Punches, &c.

Fig. 1.
ELECTRO-PLATED CUP MIXERS.
Made in two sizes,
21/- and 25/- per pair.

E.P. Cup Mixer with Strainer Top,
£1 10 0.

Fig. 2.
WHEEL MIXER,
LATEST AMERICAN PATTERNS.

Sets securely on the glass, and a slight turn of the wheel thoroughly mixes the Beverage.

Price 12/6

THE "IMPERIAL" MIXER.

As used
BY THE LEADING BARS IN THE UNITED STATES.

FIXES TO FLOOR.

EASILY OPERATED.

MIXES ALL KINDS OF BEVERAGES PERFECTLY.

Price £2 15 0

COOLING CUPS AND DAINTY DRINKS.

A COLLECTION OF RECIPES FOR SUMMER DRINKS.

Price 2/6

Mixers for all occasions

A page from L. Lumley's trade catalogue illustrating necessary bar tools. Straws are mentioned in the 1855 edition of Eliza Acton's book *Modern Cookery*. She comments on the preparation of a Mint Julep that . . . 'We apprehend that this preparation is, like most other iced American beverages, to be imbibed through a reed . . .'

REQUISITES FOR AMERICAN AND ICED DRINKS.

PATENT ROTARY ICE SHAVER.

Fig. 1.

It is **easily** operated, simple in construction, durable, and clean in use.

The opening in this Machine is five inches in diameter, and will take a piece of ice of any shape.

The knives can be adjusted to cut coarse or fine, as desired.

The entire Machine is galvanized, and will not rust or discolor the ice.

PRICE ... £1 15 0

ICE CRUSHING MACHINE.

Fig. 2.

Japanned 11/- & **15/-**

Tinned, 12/- & **16/-**

By the use of this Machine large or small quantities of Ice can be broken in the most expeditious manner. It is neat in appearance, and has no complicated parts to get out of order. Made in two sizes.

ICE SHAVES.

'Fig. 3.

Galvanized Top, fitted on Hard Wood Base, 10/-.

Fig. 4.

A simple and efficient tool for shaving Ice from Blocks, fitted with adjustable knife and hinged cover.
Galvanized   ·   · 2/-

1, America Square, Minories, London, E.C.

Ice did not always come in cubes

75

'The very latest Tells–U–How cocktail shaker' as advertised in a 1930s Asprey catalogue

An exploded view of an American cocktail shaker

A glass cocktail shaker with silver plated mounts, showing the recipes on the side

Gives ingredients for mixing the following 15 Cocktails:

ALEXANDER
BACARDI
BETWEEN THE
        SHEETS
BRONX
CLOVER CLUB
DRY MARTINI
DUBONNET
GIN RICKEY

SIDE CAR
MANHATTAN
OLD FASHIONED
ORANGE BLOSSOM
PALM BEACH
TOM COLLINS
WHISKY SOUR

—

Finest Silver Plated with Gilt Moveable Lining and Top

TELLS·U·HOW COCKTAIL SHAKER
£3 10 0 each

A silver plated shaker with
a container for freezing salts

For perfect lift off. A
standard and a miniature
cocktail shaker in the form
of Zeppelins. The base of
each unscrews to reveal
four tumblers

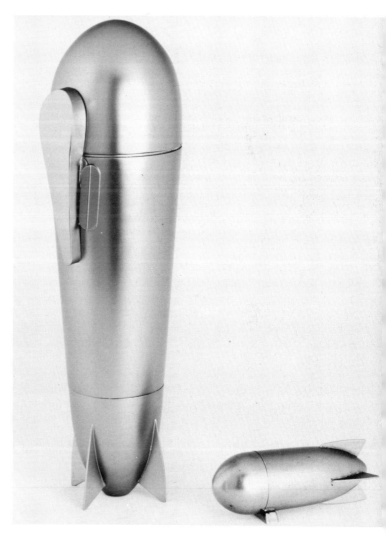

To mix complex cocktails at home while entertaining
friends to witty conversation is not necessarily an easy
task. But with a little practice, self-control can be
maintained, if everything is to hand

Asprey cocktail cabinets of
the thirties

ASPREY & CO., LTD.

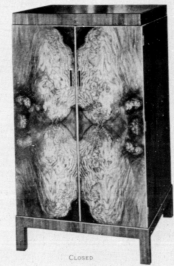

WALNUT COCKTAIL CABINET

WITH VERY FINELY FIGURED LID
AND DOORS

ELECTRIC LIGHT IN LID WHICH
OPERATES WHEN OPENED

CLOSED

FITTED WITH FINEST SILVER
PLATED COCKTAIL SHAKER AND
ENGLISH CUT GLASS

8 TUMBLERS
24 COCKTAIL GLASSES

BLACK GLASS SHELF FOR MIXING,
WITH LARGE DRAWER AND CUP-
BOARD BELOW FOR BOTTLES, ETC.
BLACK GLASS AND CHROMIUM TRAY

£49 0 0

OPEN

A sixteenth-century picnic during a Royal hunt. Drink is provided in sizeable flasks that can be refilled from the cask

CHAPTER IX

On the Move

'When you behold our barons and knights going on a military expedition, you see their baggage horses loaded, not with iron but wine, not with lances but cheeses, not with swords but bottles, not with spears but spits. You would imagine they were going to prepare a great feast, rather than to make war' – extract from a letter written by Peter of Blois [twelfth century].

Drinking is not always confined to the home, bar or club. Travelling man must have sustenance. The earth may have shrunk in terms of the time it takes to travel from one side to the other, but man's desire to make merry while on the move has continued unabated.

A Rolls-Royce with a fold-out picnic table and padded bumper seats

Childhood memories of picnics are often of some pastoral idyll. Reality is often different. The dog sits in the food, flies drive the picknicker to distraction, a bottle breaks in transit or some luckless creature forgets a vital piece of equipment.

The successful picnic requires the planning skills of a crusade and several willing helpers.

Unpacking for a Pic-Nic.

Oh! dear here's the sherry and mix'd pickles broke!
O yes, and they have broke into the pastry too.

Picnic as portrayed by
James Seymour, c. 1835

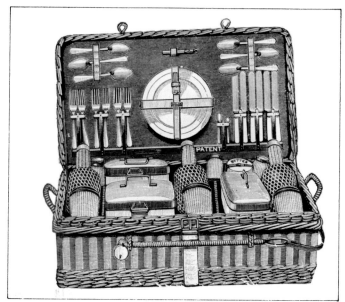

A 1930s Asprey picnic hamper with wicker covered bottles

Pocket silver nutmeg graters. Mulled wine, ale and hot toddy were all spiced with nutmeg, but tavern keepers were loth to part with either nutmeg or grater. Consequently, the customer carried his own

Bonnie Prince Charlie's
Campaign canteen found
on the battlefield of
Culloden in 1746

Outdoor drinking is not the same without a cup or beaker and preferably a nest of cups so that solace can be offered to others. Retain the largest cup for personal use

Left: A nest of 11 wooden cups, made in the seventeenth century

A rare George III double beaker

Flasks come in a variety of shapes and sizes to suit different needs

A pigskin leather/glass flask

A gold flask

A silver plated collapsible cup in a pigskin case

Above: A nest of 6 horn beakers in a pigskin case

Left: A huntsman's holster flask

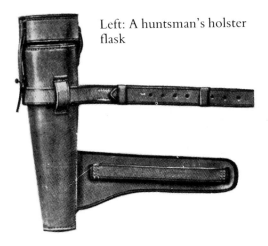

A hunting lunch case with flask

A Sussex cider press in
1898. Cider is one of the
oldest of British drinks.
The Romans discovered the
Britons were making cider
from wild apples

CHAPTER X

Brew it Yourself

Brewing and distilling have not always been the domain of big business. In the Highlands of Scotland, distilling malt whisky at home was part of each family's daily routine until legislation was introduced in 1784. Every self-respecting Highlander knew how to make malt whisky from his own barley. It was as natural to have in his home as milk and he considered the operation of a still to be his birthright. Not surprisingly, therefore, Highlanders blithely ignored the law and there were many hair-raising encounters between smugglers and excisemen. In 1823 there were 14,000 official detections of illicit stills and yet over half the whisky sold in the Lowlands came from an illicit source.

Equally, the brewing of ale and beer was an English household tradition. Each parish used to brew ale to celebrate festival days and the profits from its sale went back to the Parish. But brewing at home is a skill largely lost. The eighteenth century rural economist, William Cobbett, was outraged at its demise. Tea, he wrote, was the villain. 'I view the tea drinking as a destroyer of health, an enfeebler of the frame, an engenderer of effeminacy and laziness, a debaucher of youth and a maker of misery for old age.'

Trying to change people's lifestyles by suppressing a legitimate human desire, had the same effect on Americans as it did on the Scots. The advent of prohibition in the USA on 17th January 1920 encouraged the establishment of a massive 'Do It Yourself' drinks industry as well as the wholesale production of liquor by organised crime. Average citizens discovered ways of making gin in the bathtub and beer in the backyard. The required ingredients were packaged and sold in shops with the warning 'do not add sugar; if you do you will obtain a fermented drink forbidden by law.'

A nineteenth-century
domestic brewery

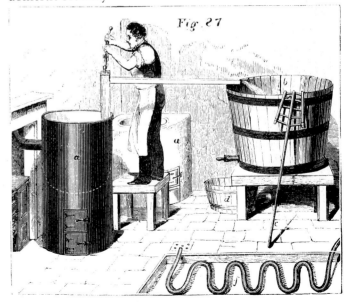

A Highland Still painted by Landseer. Alfred Barnard, author of *Whisky distilleries of the United Kingdom*, published in 1887, wrote, 'The smugglers may be looked upon as the pioneers of the whisky trade. To them is largely due the superior quality of the Fine Old Malt Whisky.'

An illicit still in Ireland

An Illinois bootlegger's still
that produced 1,500 gallons
of moonshine a day.
During prohibition, the
annual consumption of
spirits rose from 93,000,000
gallons to an estimated
300,000,000 in the USA

Senator Andrew J. Volstead, author of the Act that brought in prohibition

A daunting sight. Carry Nation, the 'Kansas Smasher', who destroyed saloons with her hatchet

A corkscrew parodying
Senator Volstead. The
worm springs out from
behind when the head is
twisted

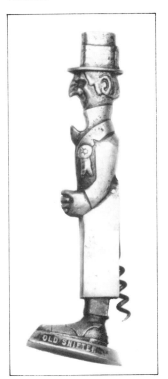

Making the consumption of
alcohol a crime turned
people into walking
cocktail cabinets

Ancient Egyptians carried
home from a drinking party

CHAPTER XI

The Morning After

Ask a scientist what effect alcohol has on the body and he will give a baffling explanation about alcohol metabolising on its journey through the system into Acetaldehyde and then Acetate, through the action of enzymes with prodigiously long names. Ask a sociologist and he will go to some length to explain that although a high intake of alcohol always has a physiological effect, a person's behaviour is largely determined by the way society tells him to behave when consuming alcohol. Ask a temperance reformer and he will launch into a sermon on morality. All this goes a long way to show that if both body and soul are taken into account, the effect on a person will be as varied as the emotional balance and character of each individual.

Thomas Young in a little book called *England's Bane*, published in 1617, listed nine types of drunkenness ranging from 'Lyon Drunke', describing a particularly quarrelsome mood, to 'Sheepe Drunke', a condition of over-zealous generosity resulting in the subject giving away the clothes on his back. Such variety is almost matched when it comes to that 'morning after' feeling. P. G. Wodehouse lists six types of hangover in a Mulliner story; The Atomic, The Broken Compass, The Cement Mixer, The Comet, The Gremlin Boogie and The Sewing Machine.

The first hangover inevitably took place very shortly after the discovery of intoxicating liquor. No one knows when this was. Anecdote has it that an ancient Persian monarch, fond of the grape, stored a quantity of unfermented grape juice in a large vessel. The juice subsequently fermented and the monarch, knowing nothing about wine, had the vessel labelled 'Poison'. However, a lady from the monarch's harem attempted suicide by drinking some of the liquid and far from dying found her spirits strangely uplifted. She continued to drink until she passed out. Of course, the next morning she awoke with a sore head and a raging thirst, whereupon she drank some more and felt much better, thus making history twice over with the first ever hangover and the first use of a 'hair of the dog'.

To treat a hangover is not merely a matter of dealing with the physical consequences, but also with blurred memories that begin to return as amnesia retreats and the awesome embarrassment of one's behaviour the night before rushes in like a spring tide. One of the most 'compleat' of imbibers, Kingsley Amis, respected novelist and famous drinker, gives the following advice on hangovers – 'Immediately on waking, start telling yourself how lucky you are to be feeling so bloody awful. This, known as George Gale's paradox, recognises the truth that if you do not feel bloody awful after a hefty night then you are still drunk, and must sober up in a waking state before hangover dawns!'

Some branded hangover treatments

'Elixir Végétal', made by
the monks of Chartreuse
from a formula dating back
to the sixteenth century and
containing the extract of
139 herbs and spices. Only
three monks know the
formula

Harris's patent Pick-me-up,
displaying the Queen
Mother's Royal Warrant.
Take care when opening the
bottle as the smell is enough
to knock a grown man
backwards

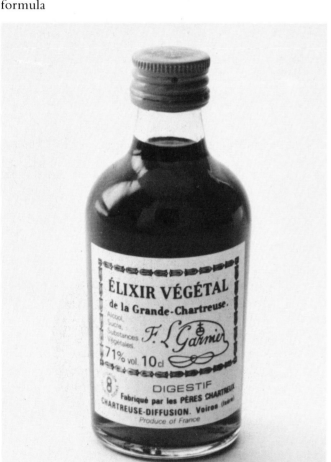

Right: Underberg is
supplied in 20 ml, one-dose
bottles and contains 44%
volume alcohol in which
the herbal ingredients are
macerated
Below: Fernet–Branca, the
world famous bitters and a
particularly effective
hangover antidote when
mixed with vodka, lemon,
sugar and ice

'Resolve', a product
recently launched by
Beecham specifically for
that 'morning after' feeling

Unicum bitters, a versatile
apéritif, digestif and
'morning after' soother

Acknowledgements

The author and the publishers acknowledge permission to reproduce the photographs in this book from the following:

Antique Collector magazine (Alistair Sampson): 84. Asprey & Co Ltd: 36, 37, 38, 39, 40, 41, 42, 44, 46, 54, 55, 56, 57, 58, 76, 77, 78, 79, 82, 85. Author's Collection: 25. Barnes Wine Shop: 16. Beecham Proprietaries: 95. Brian Beet: 43. Martin Bennett: 81. H. Blankley & Son: 10. The John Johnson Collection of Labels at the Bodleian Library: 6, 68, 71. The British Library: 51, 89, 90, 91. By Courtesy of the Trustees of the British Museum: 48, 49, 52, 53. Cadbury Schweppes PLC: 72, 73. Christie's: 9, 18, 19, 20, 21, 22, 32, 36, 44, 45, 58, 83. Mary Evans Picture Library: 17, 62, 63, 80, 82, 86, 87. The Worshipful Company of Goldsmiths: 14, 45. John Harvey & Sons: 11, 27. Jeanette Hayhurst Fine Glass: 56, 59. Heublein Inc: 32. Mrs T. Hughes: 82. Richard Kihl: 34. Macallan-Glenlivet Ltd: 32. Manchester Polytechnic Library: 13, 29, 61, 64, 65, 74, 75. The Mansell Collection: 62, 67, 73, 92. The Methuen Collection: 47. Moët et Chandon: 15, 30, 31. The Museum of London: 8, 35, 50. General Research Division of the New York Public Library, Astor, Lenox and Tilden Foundations: 90. The Northampton Museum: 9. Keith and Robert Osborne: 28. The Patent Office: 12, 13, 18. Phillips Auctioneers: 19, 21, 91. Pimms Ltd: 33. The Ritz Hotel: 66. The Röhss Museum of Arts and Crafts, Gothenburg: 50. The Royal Commission on the Historical Monuments of England: 60. Sotheby's: 22, 23, 32, 33, 59, 77, 84. By Courtesy of the Board of Trustees of the Victoria & Albert Museum: 24, 26. The Wellington Museum: 88.